ITALY
TRAVEL FOR KIDS

www.dinobibi.com
Written by: Celia Jenkins
Editor: Kristy Elam
Illustrator: Jacqueline Cacho

CONTENTS

Native Plants & Animals (pg. 22)

Food, Culture, & Traditions (pg. 26)

Famous People (pg. 38)

LEONARDO

Major Cities & Attractions (pg. 42)

INTRODUCTION: HELLO FRIENDS!

Buon giorno! It's a beautiful morning, and I'm sitting in my favourite place, in a tree. If anyone could see me now, I'm sure they'd say "Si, there goes that crazy Gaia, sitting in her tree again." But I don't care. This tree is where I come to be by myself and to think. I also come here to write in peace and quiet. I don't have a big family, but sometimes it feels very noisy.

My family isn't what you'd call an ordinary family. To start with, I'm a twin. My sister, Elena, is one hour older than me, but she thinks she's a million years wiser. She drives me nuts! Sisters, right? Elena is a name from Greek mythology. It's the Italian version of Helen, who was the daughter of Zeus. He was a God. Helen was supposed to be the most beautiful woman in the world. My name is from Greek mythology, too. Gaia was a goddess. She was the mother earth goddess, and so my name means earth.

Usually, twins get on well together, no? Not me and Elena. We have another sister who is much younger than us. Aurora is only five. My parents really loved ancient names! Aurora was the Roman goddess of morning, and in other places, the nickname is 'Dawn.' Papà chose the name before Aurora was born. He said she would be his ray of sunshine. Mama and Papà wanted another baby for a long time, and so she was a blessing to them. But sadly, Papà was very sick, and he died before Aurora was born. She never got to meet him.

So now, we're a team of girls, Mama, my twin sister Elena, and our little sister Aurora. That's my famiglia, my family. But it doesn't stop there. In the past, Italian families would be very big. Parents would have many children. Sometimes six, eight, or ten children! But these days, it's not common to have more than two. Mama was an only child. My Nonno and Nonna wanted a big family, but they only had Mama. They hoped to have many children but they just had one. I bet they were disappointed! Just like Mama, my Nonna lost her husband very early. I never met my Nonno. But Nonna came from a big family. My grandmother has four sisters and two brothers! Seven children! I think that's way too many. Even having just two siblings is sometimes too many for me.

We didn't always live here in Martina Franca. After Papà died, we moved here to be in Mama's hometown. She couldn't look after twin girls and a baby all by herself! My Nonna and Nonno had built a big house in the country-side because they wanted many children. Although their dream didn't come true, the house is full of children now! So, my sisters and my mother and I live with my grandma. Nonna's house is amazing. I was about eight years old when we came here. At first, I didn't like it, but now I love it. What's even better is that many of Nonna's siblings still live in Martina Franca, too. I spend a lot of time with my aunties and uncles.

Nonna's big house is surrounded by olive groves. She used to do nearly all the work herself with the help of Nonno. Now she hires local workers and volunteers to come and harvest the olives. When the volunteers arrive, the house is noisier than ever! Nonna gives them a place to stay and food to eat. In return, they work for free. The system works well for both of them, but it makes my life a bit chaotic. Also, not all the volunteers speak Italian. Sometimes the volunteers try to teach me their languages instead.

Nonna wanted Mama to work making olive oil too, but Mama didn't want to do that. When she was young, Mama wanted to be a model and wear beautiful clothes. But she decided to work making clothes instead. Martina Franca has a long history of producing textiles. A lot of family businesses near here make fabric and use the fabric to make wonderful clothes. Mama found a small company where the owner had no children of her own. She learned the trade and has been working hard as a textile manufacturer ever since. Sometimes Mama makes outfits for us, too.

Fun Fact
Martina Franca is a town in the province of Taranto, Apulia, southern Italy.

My whole family is Roman Catholic. Nonna is a strict Catholic, but Mama isn't so strict and doesn't make us go to church every week. Vatican City, where the Pope lives, is in Italy. So, I guess it makes sense that there are a lot of Christian people here. I'm not sure what I think yet. Maybe there's a God and maybe there's not... I don't know. Something that annoys me is that I can't find out about other religions. I have a pen friend in the UK. She told me that her religious studies teacher tells her about all different religions. In Italy, we only learn about Christianity. Right now, I go to Scuola secondaria di primo grado, which is lower secondary school. Maybe when I go to upper secondary school, my religious studies classes will be more interesting!

Fun Fact
Due to a growing population of immigrants, other religions in Italy include Judaism, Sikhism, Bhuddism, Hinduism and Islam.

Before we continue our trip, I would like to know more about you.
Can you please complete this little questionnaire for me?

Your name:

Which country are you from:

Who are you traveling with?

Which places in Italy are you most exicited about? Why?

GEOGRAPHY OF ITALY

So... Italia! What can I tell you about my wonderful country? First, do you know what Italy looks like? The shape of Italy is famous because it looks like something you will recognize. Italy looks like a boot! Not a modern boot, an old-fashioned boot that would go over your knee. Down in the south where I live is the heel. The toe is kicking towards the island of Sicily. Rome is in the middle of the boot. Up north, that's the top of the boot where you put in your foot. Look at a map of Italy. Can you see it? I think it's pretty cool.

Do you know any famous cities in Italy? I already told you that my Papà used to work in Venice. It's one of the most famous cities in Italy. So many people go on holiday to Venice. It's a popular place to propose if you want to get married. But my Nonna says that, now there are so many tourists, it's not a romantic place anymore. The nearest city to us is Bari, which has about 325,000 people living there. But that's not so big. The next biggest city near us is Naples. It's the third biggest city in Italy. Can you guess how many people live there? Almost 1 million! Naples is where I used to live before Papà died.

Fun Fact
Italy isn't the only country that looks like something. Finland looks like a rabbit. The UK looks like a dragon.

I'm sure you've heard of Rome. It's our capital city. Rome has a population of more than 2.5 million people. It's such a busy place. Although I grew up in a city, I'm not fond of busy places. Martina Franca is big enough for me! I prefer to be somewhere close to nature where I can see rivers, lakes, forests, and mountains.

I find it calming to be near water, don't you? The River Po is the longest in Italy. It measures 650 kilometers (400 miles) in length and is 500 meters (164 feet) at its width. Ok, so it's not actually very big. Compared to other rivers around the world, the River Po isn't that impressive.

The River Adige is the most interesting one in Italy. It has an underwater city! No, seriously! I'm not joking. In Curon Venosta, there's a lake that comes from the River Adige. But it's not natural; the lake is man-made. In the 1950s, they needed to make a hydroelectric plant to merge two natural lakes, but there was a town in the way. Despite protests, the local people had to move up the hill to a new town. The old one was replaced with the lake. About two-hundred houses in the Venosta Valley disappeared under the water.

Fun Fact
The belfry of the church was left behind, and it poked up out of the water on the lake.

The village of Curon Venosta isn't the only place where there's a city under water in Italy. The most famous is Fabbriche di Careggine. In the 1940s, the village was flooded. The lake was drained several times for maintenance, and you could walk around the ruins of the buildings. But they haven't drained it since 1994. I wonder if the ruin of Fabbriche di Careggine will ever see sunlight again?

Did you know that Italy has two big islands in the Mediterranean? The bit that looks like a boot is the main part of Italy. But we have two islands which aren't attached. I've already mentioned one, the island of Sicily. The other one is called Sardinia. Also, we have two sovereign states. They're in Italy but are actually enclaves — they're surrounded by Italy but not really part of it. One is the Vatican City, where the Pope lives. The other is San Marino. There's also an enclave in Switzerland called Campione d'Italia which is actually part of Italy. Confusing, right?

We have a lot of mountains in Italy. The highest point is Monte Bianco. In English, it means white mountain. Most people use the French name: Mont Blanc. It's 4,810 m tall (almost 3 miles). Our biggest lake is called Garda. Its size is 367.94 km2.

Fun Fact
Lake Garda was the site of naval battles in 1866 between Italy and Austria.

Monte Bianco

Did you know that the one of the only active volcanoes in mainland Europe is in Italy? It's famous for the destruction of the cities of Pompeii and Herculaneum in the eruption in 79 AD. That volcano's name is Vesuvius. But it's not the only active volcano in Italy. An active volcano is one that's still alive — it could still erupt. Some active volcanoes erupt all the time, and others don't erupt for hundreds or thousands of years. When a volcano hasn't erupted for 10,000 years it's called extinct. It basically means a dead volcano. The other active volcanoes in Italy are Etna, Stromboli, and Vulcano. Out of these three, Vulcano hasn't erupted in the last hundred years. Mount Etna and Mount Stromboli have continuous activity. Did you know that some islands in hills in Italy were created by volcanoes? Incredibile!

Volcanoes can be dangerous. These days, people don't often live near active volcanoes. But in the past, people chose to live near them. The soil is very good near a volcano. That means it's good for growing crops. If you live on land with fertile soil you can grow good vegetables and make a lot of money! However, if the volcano erupts, it's unlucky for you! Sometimes a volcanic eruption can make an earthquake happen. That's even more dangerous because an earthquake can affect people for miles and miles. There aren't any volcanoes near where I live, so I'm not too worried!

Currency in Italy

Italy is in Europe so we use the Euro. The cost of living depends on where you live. Of course, it's more expensive to live in a big city! Some things are cheap in Italy. For example, a coffee might be €1.30 (£1.16 / $1.47) and a liter of milk is €1.10 (£1.00 / $1.25). But of course, it depends on what you like to buy. Wherever you live, you can choose to shop cheaply or expensively!

From Coasts to Mountains, Italy's Varied Climate

Buon giorno! I'm sitting in my favourite tree again. Usually I come outside in the morning. In the afternoon, it's too hot. We live in the south of Italy so the weather can get really warm. If I come and sit here in the afternoon, I'll be baked! The morning is cool and quiet. Well, not as quiet as I'd like it to be! Over in the field are volunteers and workers picking the olives. They wake up even earlier than me to get the coolest part of the day. I like it best in the mid-morning when it's a good temperature. Not too hot and not too cool.

Italy is a nice place to be if you like varied temperatures. This country is long and thin. In the north, the temperatures are much colder. In north Italy, there are snow-capped mountains. But in the south, it's so much warmer. Sometimes it can be too warm! But if you want to escape to a different climate, you don't have to go too far. There's a big difference between the highs and lows of our climate.

Fun Fact
In Italy, the highest and lowest temperatures ever recorded are -45°C (-50F) in the Italian Alps and 46°C (114F) in the far south.

In the mountainous regions in the north, it can be snowy all year round. I don't think I'd like that! It's fun to see snow once in a while. But if it was snowy every day, I'd get sick of it. It must be tiring wearing thick, warm clothes all the time, don't you think? I prefer to wear summer clothes that are light and breezy. In the north, there are a lot of mountains which are more than 4,000 meters (over 2 miles) tall. That's why it's so snowy there. There's Mont Blanc, Monte Rosa, and Gran Paradiso. Those places are popular for skiing. At the top of the mountains, it's always cold. But if you go down the mountains, temperatures are warmer in the summer.

For example, Turin is at the foot of the Alps. Because it's near the mountains, it can get very cold. However, the summers can be warm. So, it has a big difference across the seasons. In Turin, it can be 27°C (80°F) in the summer, and -2°C (28°F) at night

time in the winter. Milan is another city in the north, but it's not so close to the mountains. As such, their temperatures in the summer can be warmer than Turin. In Milan, it can be around 29°C (84°F) in the summer, and -1°C (30°F) in the winter. So, Milan and Turin are similar. But both places experience a lot of rainfall. The higher up the mountain you go, the rainier it gets!

Fun Fact

If you don't like rain, the best time to visit Milan is in September.

But what about Venice? It's probably in the top three most popular places to visit in Italy, so I guess you want to know about that one! Venice is also in the north but on the east side. So, I think the temperatures won't be the same as Turin or Milan. Venice isn't mountainous, it's coastal. Everyone thinks that Venice is an island. Actually, only some of the city is built on an island. Some areas like Marghera and Favaro Veneto aren't on islands at all. But anyway, because most of Venice is on islands, the temperatures are cool and breezy. Temperatures in Venice range from 28°C (82°F) in the summer, and 0°C (32°F) in the winter. You might have expected it to be warmer than that in the summer, right? But don't forget about the bora, which is a cold wind blowing from the plains of Eastern Europe. It makes the air chilly, so it doesn't get so warm.

Fun Fact

As well as the bora, Venice is also plagued by acqua alta, which is high water that floods the city.

As you can see, there's quite a variety of climates across Italy! We have polar, cold, temperate, and arid climates across our diverse country. I think it's wonderful to live in a diverse place. It means there's something for everyone. You can go skiing in the snow. You can swim in warm Mediterranean Sea. You can relax on cool, coastal places with light breezes. So, if you can travel around you can experience whatever weather you prefer.

However, like a lot of places, Italy is experiencing change. Global warming means that temperatures are changing. The hotter weather means that the glaciers are melting. Without glaciers there is no snow and no skiing! When the glaciers melt, it also makes the sea level rise. This isn't good news either. How long will it be before Venice is under water? It's not just the Venetian islands. Many of our cultural hot spots are low-lying which means they will easily flood if the sea level rises. Finally, our poor crops won't survive if the heat continues to rise. Italy is famous for delicious wine. But grapes need a very specific temperature to grow well. If the grapes can't grow then we can't make wine any more.

So, it's a big worry for all of us. Nonna doesn't grow grapes but she grows olives, so she's concerned about the temperature rises too. We live in the countryside and don't have a very technological lifestyle. Nonna's house is traditional. We don't have a television in every room or bright lights on all the time. We often use candles at dinnertime and try to use less electricity than before. It's only a small contribution, but if everyone does what they can then I'm sure the planet will appreciate it!

Ancient Theatre of Taormina in Sicily, built in 300BC.

Ciao, mio amico! Hello, my friend! If you like history, Italy is a great place to start. That's because Italy is sort of where history began. I'm serious! In Casa Belvedere, which is in Monte Poggiolo, archaeologists have found some old artifacts. They're thought to be Paleolithic era, so they are around 850,000 years old.

There's a lot of stuff in Italy that's really old. A while ago, Mama took a pottery class and wanted to make something in the Cardium ware style.

Cardium pottery is a Neolithic decorative style used in pottery. Its name comes from the cockle shell that's used to make the pattern in the clay. That type of pottery was made across Italy and dates back to 6,000 BC. Of course, there isn't a lot of original Cardium pottery left. After 8,000 years, it isn't hard to imagine how many pieces got broken! But sometimes people like to make new pottery in the same style. That sort of rustic, naïve style goes and in and out of fashion all the time.

The next historical thing I want to tell you about is kinda gross. I hope you're not squeamish! My sister Elena doesn't like yucky stuff. But I think this story is cool so I want to tell you anyway. It's about Ötzi. The Ötztal Alps are on the border between Italy and Austria. In 1991, something really yucky was found. A body! But it wasn't a recent body. They found the body of a man who lived around 3,400 BC. They called the man Ötzi because of where they found him. He was found by two German tourists who were hiking. The body was frozen into the glacier, so they took a picture to show the authorities.

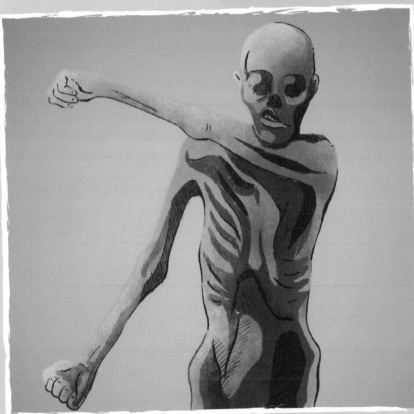

When the body was recovered, they found out how old Ötzi was. For a long time, nobody could discover how he had died. Eventually, scientists announced that Ötzi was probably killed in a fight. They found an arrowhead in his left shoulder which made him bleed to death. There were other wounds on his body that told them he'd been fighting. Also, scientists could find the blood of at least four other people on Ötzi's knife and coat.

Fun Fact
Ötzi is the oldest discovered natural skeleton of a Copper Age man in Europe.

I think that ancient history is the most interesting of all. If something happened just 50 or 100 years ago, we know so much about it. We can read letters, see photographs and films, and maybe even speak to people who were there. But for ancient history there are so many more gaps to fill. You have to be a real detective to know anything about the distant past. Maybe I'm just interested because my name is from Greek mythology. Have you ever met anyone called Gaia before? My sister's name, Elena, is a bit more common, no?

If you think that Greek mythology is only to do with Greece, you're wrong. Actually, there are many things from Greek mythology which have links with Italy, too. For example... the Trojan War. Yes, the same one with the famous horse. The Trojan War started because Paris (the Prince of Troy) took Helen of Sparta (who Elena is named after) away from her husband. Although actually, the war started because of all these women arguing about who was the most beautiful. There were three goddesses called Hera, Athena, and Aphrodite. They asked Paris who was the fairest. He said it was Aphrodite. In return, she made Helen of Troy fall in love with Paris, even though she was already married to the King of Troy. So that's where all the trouble started. Anyway... what was I saying? Oh yes, this story has links to Italy. Aphrodite had a son called Aeneas. He was a Trojan hero and led the surviving Trojans from the war to... can you guess? That's right, to Italy.

There's a link in the story between me and my sister. In the story with the three goddesses, Paris chooses the winner by giving her a golden apple. So, Helen (Elena) of Troy fell in love with Paris because Aphrodite got a golden apple. There's another famous golden apple in Greek mythology. The mother goddess, who was called Gaia, gave a golden apple as a gift too. She gave the apple to Hera and Zeus as a wedding present.

I'm sure you know that Rome is the capital of Italy. But do you know when it was founded? Or who by? I'll start at the beginning... In an ancient Latin city called Alba Longa, the daughter of a displaced king gave birth to twin boys. I like stories with twins! The new king didn't want anything to threaten his throne. He commanded that they boys were killed. They were left to die at the side of a river. However, the boys, Romulus and Remus, survived. A she-wolf gave them milk so they wouldn't starve. While they were still babies, the two boys were rescued by a shepherd. They grew up on a farm and helped with the sheep. They knew nothing about their past.

When the boys were adults, there was a local argument about the king. This king was the same one who had stolen the throne from their grandfather. But of course, Romulus and Remus didn't know it at the time. Remus went to prison because he joined in the argument about the king. Romulus tried to free his brother. At this time, their grandfather (the rightful king) and their uncle (the bad king) realized who these two men were. Eventually, Romulus could free his brother, and their uncle was killed. Their grandfather was the king again.

Knowing who they were, Romulus and Remus decided to build their own city and rule over it. However, the twin brothers couldn't agree on where to build it. Maybe it's common for twins to fight? They had a fight and Romulus killed Remus. This event was in the year 753 BC and was the beginning of Rome. Isn't it a crazy story? Many writers have written about this myth and some say there might even be some truth to the story.

Fun Fact

Romulus was King of Rome for nearly forty years and then he disappeared in a whirlwind!

I'm so excited about today! Liliana is coming to take me for an outing. Do you remember that I said my Nonna has six siblings? Most of them still live in Martina Franca. Her youngest sister is Liliana, and she's my favourite aunty. Liliana is about ten years younger than Nonna and doesn't seem anything like a grandma! Actually, Liliana never got married and never had children. When I asked her about it, she said she was more interested in having a good career! Liliana is a Biodiversity Research Consultant. Her job is to check which animals are living in different places and advise people and companies on how to encourage more animals.

I used to be afraid of wild animals but now I love them. Liliana has taught me so much about creatures and critters. Sometimes we go for a walk, just us, and she shows me a lot of animals I never would have noticed. Do you think about animals when you think about Italy? Maybe you should, because Italy has the most faunal biodiversity in Europe. That means it has a more varied mix of animals than anywhere else in Europe! Isn't that crazy?

One reason why we have such a range is because Italy is a mixed country. It's cold and snowy in the north. But it's warm and humid in the south. So, we can support many different animals. Many of our unique animals are small, but that doesn't mean they aren't important. I used to like big animals like elephants. We don't have wild elephants in Italy, of course! Liliana has encouraged me to appreciate small animals, too. I know all about the small creatures we can find in the country. You can even see them in your garden!

The Italian hare is a special bunny rabbit we have here in Italy. It's smaller than other types of rabbit. The best place to see the hare is on Sicily. That's an island, and so there aren't many predators for this cute creature. Another small animal is the Apennine shrew. Do you know what a shrew is? They look a bit like a mouse, but they're not very similar! A mouse can be white, brown, grey, or black. But a shrew will only be grey. Also, mice are mostly vegetarian; they eat grass, roots, leaves, and seeds. But shrews eat different things; they eat beetles, crickets, vegetation, and small animals like small birds, snakes, or even mice!

Liliana has a special interest in toads and frogs. Most girls think toads are yucky. Not me! I'd love to have a frog for a pet, but I think Elena would cry! About 40 species of amphibians live in Italy. One of my favourite frogs is the common parsley frog. They are speckled in all different shades of green. The Italian tree frog is cool as well. They're such a bright green colour!

Fun Fact

One type of salamander that can only be found in Italy is the Sardinian mountain newt. However, due to threats of pollution, and other disturbances to its habitat, it has been classified as endangered species.

23

Ok, you know I said we don't have elephants in Italy? Well, we used to! In Sicily and Sardinia, a long, long time ago, we had elephants. We're talking prehistoric, of course. That means pre-history... or before history. Over 3 million years ago. The elephants that lived here were dwarf elephants. That's because living in this part of the work wasn't really suitable, so the elephants got smaller and smaller. Eventually, they died out. Fossils have survived, so we can study them.

I wonder where Liliana will take me today. Sometimes we go walking in the countryside. Sometimes she takes me to a zoo or museum. Across Italy, there are about twenty National Parks. I've been to a few of them with Liliana. Sometimes my twin sister Elena comes with us, but she's not really interested in animals. We have many regional parks as well. I've been to marine reserves with Liliana, too. I want to go to more zoological museums, but there aren't any near here. They're all in big cities like Milan, Rome, Turin, and Pisa.

These days, the flora and fauna in Italy is under threat. This problem isn't just for Italy, but the whole world, I think. Also, it's not a new problem. Deforestation and destruction of nature in Italy started in Roman times. But now we're more aware and try to focus on conservation. Did you know that Italy is a signatory to the Berne Convention? That means that Italy has joined other countries and promised to help the environment. The main thing it does is tries to protect natural habitats and endangered species in our countries. I think it's important for countries to work together so we can help the planet.

We have so many nice trees, plants, flowers, and shrubs in Italy. I want to protect them. One of my favourite shrubs is called the Common Broom. Its Latin name is Cytisus scoparius. This shrub has bright yellow flowers that grow on its tall stem. When I was little, I called it the sunshine plant. It looks like a ray of sunshine!

Nonna's favourites are evergreen plants. That means they're green and have leaves all year round. They're forever-green. Cool name, isn't it? Did you know that citrus fruits are part of the evergreen vegetation family? Oranges, limes, lemons... citrus fruits are delicious. Lemon is an important flavour in Italian cooking. We use it to season and give flavour to both sweet and savoury dishes. It's common to see field upon field of lemon trees in Italy. In some places, lemon trees can only be grown in warm greenhouses. But in Italy, our temperate climate means they can grow outside. If you walk past a field of lemon trees, you'll smell them instantly!

Common broom

Ciao! It's me, Gaia. There are so many people here today! Do you remember I told you that volunteers help Nonna on her farm? They come from all over the world and stay with us while they work. Today, three new volunteers arrived. These three are all from Italy, but none of them are Italian. Does that surprise you? In Italy there are many foreigners who have come to live here. About 92% of the population is Italian. So, we have over 5 million foreign residents here. When Mama was younger, there weren't so many foreigners in Italy. Foreigners started coming to Italy in the 1980s. A lot of these people came from Eastern Europe. The three volunteers who joined us today are from Romania, Albania, and Poland. It is fun having different people around!

I like it when we have foreigners come to visit. Although there are many foreigners who live in Italy, I don't see them often. That's because about 87% of foreigners in Italy live in economically developed areas such as the north and centre of Italy. Down here in the south east we don't see so many foreigners. But it's a beautiful area, so foreign people like to visit. I think that there are many things people like about Italy.

Fun Fact
Romanians in Italy number about one million.

Architecture is very important to Italian culture. We love beautiful buildings and take care of old things around the country. Italy was the birthplace of many architectural styles, such as Baroque, Renaissance, and Neoclassical. Important Italian landmarks are recognized all over the world. For example, you can't fail to recognize the Leaning Tower of Pisa, the Coliseum, and St Peter's Basilica. The Byzantine Empire was a period in our history when many beautiful buildings were constructed. Byzantine style has a lot of glamorous gold, round archways, and impressive domed ceilings. When you're enjoying architecture in Italy, always remember to look up!

Fun Fact
One of the best ceiling views in Italy is the Sistine Chapel in Vatican City.

We have many traditions in Italy and some of them might seem a little strange. I think foreign visitors want to join in with our traditions, but they don't know much about them. So, I'll tell you what I know! First, I'd like to start with the Venetian masks. These are the famous carnival masks that almost every tourist buys in Venice. Do you ever wonder why people wear these masks? The answer is simple; to protect their identity. It's a disguise. People would wear the masks when they went to parties. If they wore a mask it made them feel free. They could do what they wanted, and people wouldn't be able to see who they were. Also, wearing a mask meant that people were more equal. You could be a servant or a prince, and nobody would know which if you were wearing a mask!

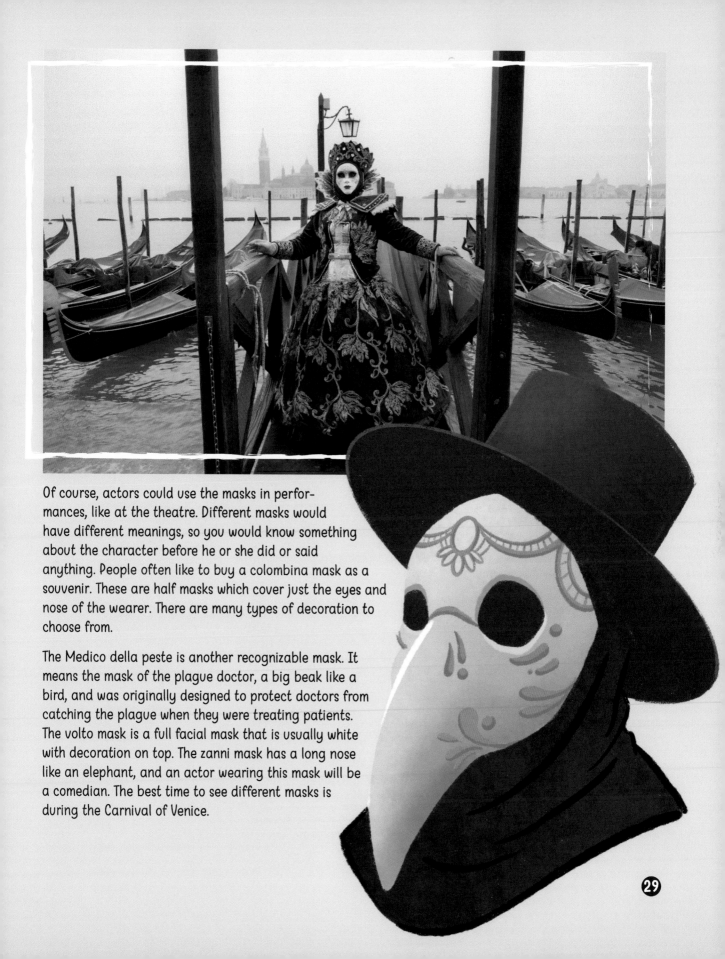

Of course, actors could use the masks in performances, like at the theatre. Different masks would
have different meanings, so you would know something
about the character before he or she did or said
anything. People often like to buy a colombina mask as a
souvenir. These are half masks which cover just the eyes and
nose of the wearer. There are many types of decoration to
choose from.

The Medico della peste is another recognizable mask. It
means the mask of the plague doctor, a big beak like a
bird, and was originally designed to protect doctors from
catching the plague when they were treating patients.
The volto mask is a full facial mask that is usually white
with decoration on top. The zanni mask has a long nose
like an elephant, and an actor wearing this mask will be
a comedian. The best time to see different masks is
during the Carnival of Venice.

We have some strange traditions in Italy which people don't really believe these days, but the custom still exists. For example, Nonna won't take a bath if she feels sick. It's a tradition that if you take a bath when you feel unwell, people think it will make you even more sick! Also, Nonna is superstitious about bread. A loaf of bread is, for religious people, a symbol of life. As such, they won't put a loaf of bread upside down because its bad luck. And you can't just pay attention to where you put your bread, you also have to pay attention to where you put your hat! In Italy, it's unlucky to put a hat on a bed. Why? I have no idea!

Castel del Monte is a Unesco World Heritage Site.

Fun Fact
Another religious supersti-tion says that you should lay objects together in the shape of a cross.

So, what do you think about the culture and traditions of Italy? We're a unique country and have many things to see. Did you know that Italy has more UNESCO World Heritage Sites than any other country in the world? It's true! We have a long history, and all our cultural relics come from different periods. Art, literature, music, architecture... there are many things we can offer. How many monuments are there in Italy? Can you guess? A monument is anything from a museum or a palace to a villa or a historical house. In Italy, we have over 100,000 monuments! If you saw one monument every day, it would take you nearly 300 years to see them all. So, I suggest that you just pick your favourites.

The thing about having a twin is that you always have to share your birthday. Parties are for both of us, and sometimes we get joint presents too. Elena and I are twins but we're quite different. For example, Elena likes girly things like make-up and pretty dresses and painting pictures. An ideal birthday party for Elena would involve dancing, and she would only invite girls! My ideal party would be an adventure in a zoo or activity centre where I can run around and get muddy. Or maybe I'd like to eat a meal in a foreign restaurant and try something new. But Elena has food allergies and doesn't like trying new things. It's so unfair! We always have to do something that Elena likes.

I'm thinking about birthdays because tomorrow is Aurora's birthday. She will be six years old. Birthdays are supposed to be a happy time, but Aurora's birthday always makes me sad. It reminds me how many years it's been since Papà passed away. Another birthday that Papà will miss. But I try to be cheerful because Aurora is little. I know Mama finds birthdays a stressful time, too. In other countries, you might pay to attend a birthday party. For example, if you go out for a meal or you go to the cinema, you might have to give some money to attend. But in Italy, the person with the birthday (or their parents!) pay for everything. Mama only has three children, which isn't as many as people used to have, but birthdays can be expensive. Nonna always helps with the preparations. This afternoon I will be helping Nonna bake the birthday cake. I think Mama is dreading the time when Elena and I turn 18. In Italy, the eighteenth birthday party is the most important. Usually you will invite at least 100 guests, or maybe 200 or 300! It's not a good time to have twins!

Birthday traditions in Italy aren't that different to other places. We have a cake with candles on, presents, and a party. Is it the same for you? But we have other celebrations that are different to other places. For example, most people think that witches are for Halloween and Father Christmas is for Christmas time, right? Not in Italy. Let me introduce you to La Befana. She's a witch, but she's not scary. La Befana is a friendly witch who does nice things.

Fun Fact
La Befana is an old woman who wears a black shawl, and she is often covered in soot from the fireplace.

Birthday traditions in Italy aren't that different to other places. We have a cake with candles on, presents, and a party. Is it the same for you? But we have other celebrations that are different to other places. For example, most people think that witches are for Halloween and Father Christmas is for Christmas time, right? Not in Italy. Let me introduce you to La Befana. She's a witch, but she's not scary. La Befana is a friendly witch who does nice things.

I live in the south east of Italy, and we have different traditions to the north. One local festival I love is Ballo della pupa. It's only really celebrated in the south of Italy. The festival is actually called the Patrons Festival, and Ballo della pupa is the name of a dance which happens at the end of the festival. The dancer wears a mannequin that looks like a dancing lady with a big skirt. On top of the mannequin are fireworks! When the dancer puts on the costume, they set fire to the fireworks. It's so crazy! As they dance around, sparks fly everywhere. They dance to the music of an accordion. The fireworks send glowing light all around the square, and the sparks dance across the flag stones. The last time we went, Elena cried and said it was too dangerous. She's such a baby! I love the fire dance and would love to see a pupa dance competition, where there are many dancers wearing the pupa mannequins.

There are some unusual festivals in the north of Italy, too. One is the Battle of the Oranges. Basically, there are nine teams, and they all throw oranges at each other! The festival has a long history and is a commemoration of when the city had to defend itself against a tyrant. Each of the nine teams has a name and people take it very seriously. The Battle of the Oranges takes place in March each year.

Do you remember that Nonna is quite traditional? Well, one example of this is that she still takes part in traditional Italian folk dances. Different regions have unique dances, and Nonna used to be an expert in the local dance where we live. Mama said that she used to be so embarrassed to watch her mum and dad when they danced at local festivals. Now Nonna is alone she doesn't dance so much, but sometimes they invite her to teach young people who to do the folk dances.

In Italy we take food and drink very seriously. There are some ingredients that are so important, they even have their own festival! For example, have you heard of truffles? A truffle is a type of fungus, or mushroom. Truffles are hard to grow and have to be harvested naturally, so they're very expensive. Some chefs call a truffle the 'diamond of the kitchen.' There's a type of truffle we call Truffle of the White Madonna. There's an autumn food festival called the International Alba White Truffle Festival; Fiera Internazionale del Tartufo Bianco d'Alba. At the festival you can see and buy some very expensive truffles.

Fun Fact

Truffles are harvested with the help of female pigs or dogs! They can smell the strong aroma of the mush-rooms.

Pass the Pizza, Please!

After Aurora's birthday party, I felt like I'd never want to eat cake again! I ate so much birthday cake that I was feeling really sick. Do you ever do that? In our family, we don't often eat sweet treats, so when we do, sometimes I have too much. People in Italy mostly eat cake for special occasions. We don't eat sweet snacks every day. In other countries, I know its popular to snack between meals. People might have a snack before lunch, or in the afternoon, such as cake, biscuits, or chocolate. But we don't do that often. Usually, we have three big meals and no snacks in between. If I'm hungry in the after-noon, Nonna lets me have a piece of fruit.

Do you know much about Italian food? I bet you think we eat pizza and pasta all the time, right? Well, I think you'll be shocked when you come to Italy! In Italy, we have a varied diet, and it's actually quite healthy. You might think that with eating pizza all the time, Italians would be fat. However, people in Italy are healthier than other countries. If you look at other European countries, they have much higher rates of adults being overweight and obese. Countries like Turkey, Malta, Latvia, Lithuania, and the United Kingdom have a big problem with this; more than 50% of adults are overweight. But in Italy, we have a healthier diet and so people weigh a lot less.

It's all to do with portions. If an American or British family eats an Italian meal, they'll choose a big bowl of pasta that's smothered in rich sauce and cheese, or a big, greasy pizza. We eat these things in Italy too, but not in the same quantities. For example, if Nonna makes pasta for dinner, it will be a simple dish, and we will just eat a small bowl. After that, we'll have either antipasto or secondo. Antipasto is usually a mixed platter of meat, cheese, and vegetables. Typically, we'll have black and green olives, cherry tomatoes, salami, mozzarella, artichoke, ham, figs, grilled peppers, and grilled aubergine. Many types of antipasto are stored in glass jars filled with oil, so they keep for a long time. So, this is a light, healthy dish to follow our pizza or pasta! Or, we might have secondo. This course is the second one of the meal. It will usually be meat or fish with lots of fresh vegetables. In Italy, we like to eat seasonal vegetables. That means we eat whatever is ripe at that time of year. Honestly, I think that vegetables are the most important part of Italian dining — not pizza or pasta!

For breakfast we eat something light but filling. Mama and Nonna drink coffee, and we children have some fresh juice. We eat a pastry, some bread, or brioche for breakfast. It isn't much but we need to save room for a big lunch! The lunchtime meal is the main meal of the day in Italy. We start with the primo, which is either soup, rice, or pasta. Then secondo or antipasto, and finally dolci, the pudding. We eat two or three courses at lunchtime but each course is small. That's why Italians are healthy even though we eat three course meals every day! Dinner is similar to lunch but is usually smaller. It's easier to get a good night's sleep if you're not too full. Sometimes we have cake or something special, but usually the pudding is fruit. We love fresh fruit in our house! My sister Elena likes peaches and plums, while Aurora prefers grapes. I like pears and apricots best. Nonna likes to eat figs, whereas Mama prefers cherries.

Bread with pastrami and mozzarella cheese.

Fun Fact

While you can get almost anything on a pizza these days, the original pizzas from Napoli only came in two flavours. Margherita pizza is tomato sauce, mozzarella and basil, and Mariana is tomato sauce, garlic, oregano, and olive oil. Simple!

Of course, I like pizza, but I don't eat it every day! Actually, I don't eat it every week! In Italy, pizza is something that locals like to eat with their friends in a restaurant. But it's expensive to dine out, so we just do that occasionally. Sometimes we make pizza because we have a pizza oven in the courtyard. Nonna had it built when she started getting volunteers to help with the olive harvest. Volunteers like to eat a lot! Also, volunteers from other countries want to eat a lot of pizza! So once or month, or more often if there are a lot of volunteers, we have a pizza party. All the volunteers help to make the pizza. In Italy, we don't always make round pizzas like everyone imagines. It's easier to make a big square pizza. We make a big bowl of salad and all eat together in the garden. It's good fun, and I'm so full afterwards!

We are proud of our cuisine in Italy. I like to try foreign food, but my family isn't so keen. Older generations of Italians just like to eat Italian food. Nonna isn't happy to try new things! That's because people like to grow their own food, and they're suspicious of things that come from other places. Eating isn't just functional in Italy; we really enjoy our food. Every meal is eaten at a table (or in the garden) with family and friends. Italians won't eat by themselves! We like to eat slowly and savour our food. We also like to have good conversations at dinnertime and often invite friends to dinner.

My favourite Italian treat is gelato. It's similar to ice-cream but much lower in fat. It's also much more delicious! When the weather is warm, it's so lovely to walk down the street with a cone full of gelato. You can get so many flavours these days, but Nonna won't try them, she just wants to get her favourite, which is choco-late gelato. Aurora likes chocolate flavour too. I have too many favour-ites to choose from! Pistachio, hazel-nut, panna (which means cream or custard), Stracciatella (which is vanilla with chocolate bits), and Frutti di bosco (which means fruits of the forest). Mmm… I'm in the mood for a gelato now! Perhaps if I help Nonna with the chores this evening she will take me for some gelato on the weekend!

Have you ever met somebody famous? Not me. Honestly, I'm not that bothered by celebrities. My sister Elena is completely different. She has so many boy bands that she follows and actors she's in love with. I think if she had the chance to meet her idols, she'd do anything! She's the only person in my family who is celebrity obsessed. We tease Nonna about her celebrity crush. You might have heard of him. He's an American-Italian actor called Robert De Niro. Do you know him? He's not in many films these days, but he used to be popular. Nonna said he used to be a heartthrob! His most famous films were released ages ago. Nonna has them all on DVD. Here are some of them: Goodfellas, The Godfather Part II, and The Deer Hunter. The only De Niro film I've seen is Stardust. A lot of his other films aren't suitable for children!

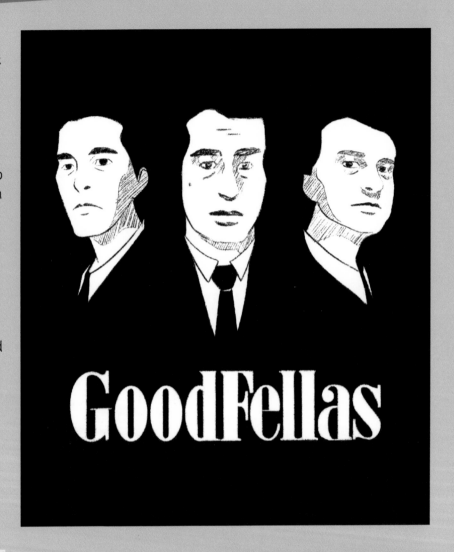

Fun Fact
De Niro's father had Italian roots, but Robert De Niro was born in America. In 2006, he was granted an Italian passport.

I don't know many modern celebrities. At least, I would only recognize American actors and singers. What about you? I bet you know more than me. I'm more interested in famous people from history. I think that's because of my best friend, Bella. She's really good at history and gets top marks on the history exam every year. She doesn't read stories about pop stars or vampires like everyone else does. Bella likes to read books all about historical figures. She's so studious!

Just recently she was telling me about an Italian luthier. Do you know what a luthier is? No, I didn't either. It's someone who makes guitars and violins. Isn't that a good job? Anyway, Bella knows all about this guy called Andrea Amati who was a luthier. As well as being a book boffin, Bella is also really skilled at playing the violin. Amati lived in the 1500s, and he basically invented the violin. Other instruments existed with three strings, but Amati made four stringed violins. His violins were smaller than the ones we have today. Bella said they were very elegant with beautiful curving scrolls; that's the twirly bit at the top. Both of his sons and his grandson were also good at making violins.

Ok, so there's something else that Bella is good at: science. She sounds super brainy, right? But you can't be good at everything. Bella is good at history, music, and science but she's terrible at math and geography. Anyway, she likes telling me all about historical scientists, too. Recently she's been researching female scientists from history because she said there isn't enough information about them, only the male scientists. She found out about a scientist from the 1300s called Dorotea Bucca. Dorotea was a physician. That basically means a doctor. She was the first female professor to be accepted onto the board of the University of Bologna. I wonder if she got a medal for it? Probably not. In the university she held a chair of medicine and philosophy for over forty years. Pretty cool for someone in the 1300s!

Celia Grillo Borromeo was a scientist and mathematician from the late 1600s. Apparently, she could solve every equation ever given to her. I can't imagine getting 100% on every math test! I'm not as bad as Bella, but math isn't my strong point! The amazing mathematician Celia could also speak eight languages! An Italian scientist from more recent times is Rita Levi-Montalcini. In 1986, she won the Nobel Prize in Physiology or Medicine. This award was because of her amazing research to do with nerve growth.

Seeing as Bella is so interested in historical people, I've been doing some research. I want to impress her with my knowledge of famous people from years gone by. But I'm not interested in science or violins, so I chose something else. I was watching a documentary about art with Nonna when I discovered an Italian painter. Her name was Artemisia Gentileschi, and she was born in 1593. It was a hard time to be a painter if you were a woman! Artemisia wasn't allowed to hire models or an art teacher. People didn't take her work seriously. But Artemisia was very talented. She worked hard to win respect and today is thought of as one of the best Italian painters. She mostly painted pictures of women and stories from the Bible.

Fun Fact

Artemisia Gentileschi was the first woman to become a member of the Accademia di Arte del Disegno in Florence and had international clientele.

One of the most famous Italian painters is Leonardo da Vinci. But he wasn't only a painter. He was also a writer, sculptor, architect, musician, inventor, scientist, mathematician, engineer, geologist (looking at rocks), anatomist (expert in the human body), cartographer (making maps), and a botanist (studying plants). Some say that da Vinci was the most talented person who has ever lived. I think I agree! I mean... what did he do to relax?

Handmade figurine of famous people with Pavaroti in the center and Rita Levi Montalcini in he lower right.

Uh-oh, Nonna has put on one of her operatic CD's. She loved listening to opera music. I just can't understand it! And I don't know why Nonna needs to listen to it so loudly. Her favourite opera singer is Luciano Pavarotti. He was a tenor which means that he could sing quite high notes for a man. Wow, his voice is so powerful!

When he died in 2007, Mama said Nonna cried for days and days. Well, I'm glad Nonna enjoys the music... but it's not for me! I think I need to escape into the garden to get away from the noise!

Fun Fact
Pavarotti was a member of one of the most famous classic singing groups of all time called The Three Tenors. The group was made up of Plácido Domingo, José Carreras, and Luciano Pavarotti.

MAJOR CITIES AND ATTRACTIONS

Do you ever have one of those days where you feel like you need a holiday? I'm having one of those days! Elena and Aurora were playing hairdressers and begged me to join in. Well, let's just say that Aurora got my hair in such a tangle that Nonna had to cut the comb out of it! Luckily the chopped hairs are at the back near my neck where you can't see them, but I'm still annoyed. Sisters! So, I've been thinking about all the places I'd like to escape to if I had the choice.

When I'm thinking about holidays I usually think of Naples. That's where I used to live before Papà died. Naples is a great city. It's the largest city in southern Italy and is just two hours from Rome. So, I think that many tourists who go to Rome also choose to visit Naples. Like a lot of place in Italy, there are many museums of interest in Naples. I rarely get to visit these because my sisters aren't interested. But my friend Bella once went to Naples with her famiglia and invited me to go too. That was one of the best holidays of my life! Bella's entire family is interested in history, so we had a great time.

Fun Fact
The Italian name for Naples is "Napoli" which comes from the Greek word Neapolis meaning "new city". The city's inhabitants are called "Neapolitans".

42

A place I like to visit in Naples is Galleria Borbonica. In English, it's called the Bourbon Tunnel. It's an ancient underground passage that connects military barracks with the Royal Palace. I don't know if any Italian royals ever used it to escape their homes, but I know it was used during WW2 as a bomb shelter. You can go for tours down there, and it's spooky. Italy has a lot of cool things underground. Do you remember I told you about those underwater towns that got flooded? Naples has other underground things you can visit. Napoli Sotterranea is forty meters underground where you can discover forgotten worlds. I like seeing the Greek-Roman Aqueduct, the Summa Cavea, and the remains of a Roman Theatre.

Underground tunnel system below the lively city of naples.

But, I'm not in the mood for a city holiday. If I could go anywhere right now, I think I'd choose a wide-open space where I could go hiking. I like enjoying nature and being outdoors. The Amalfi Coast is a great place for these activities. It's in the south of Italy so it's not far from where I am. The coastline is so blue; it's the bluest place I've ever been. Where the sea meets the sky, all you can see is blue. I like the way that the houses on the coast are piled up on top of each other, all the way up the cliff. It looks like a child had dropped their building bricks and they've fallen perfectly in place. The village of Positano is the best place on the Amalfi Coast. Every photograph looks like it could be a postcard in a shop.

Have you heard of Florence? It's a very popular place to visit. People say that Florence is one of the best places for art, museums, and architecture. The Galleria degli Uffizi is known as the Uffizi Gallery in English. People often go to this one because its near to the Piazza della Signoria in the Historic Centre of Florence. Many of the items in the museum come from the house of Medici. Do you know about them? The Medici family was a very rich, noble Italian family. So, they could afford some very nice pieces of artwork! It's fitting that these works of art should end up in Florence. This city was the birthplace of High Renaissance Art.

Just outside of Florence is a little town called Fiesole. Not many tourists know about this place. It's an expensive town, but I think it's worth visiting. There's a gorgeous church on top of a huge hill. It has a small olive grove courtyard, and its overlooking Florence, so you get an amazing view. Do you know the artist Michelangelo? He made a very famous statue called David. The marble that was used for this statue is said to have come from the village of Fiesole.

Another place you should visit near Florence is San Gimigna-no. It's only an hour away so you should really go there. It's a medieval town with a wall around the outside. Other medieval features of the town survive to this day. You can also see more modern features like Romanesque and Gothic architecture. Another reason to visit is that the gelato is amazing there!

I guess I should tell you something about our capital, too. Of course, you know what the capital is, don't you? It's Rome! All roads lead to Rome, or so they say. Everyone likes to go to the Colosseum and the Pantheon. There are famous fountains where the water sparkles in the sunlight and museums where you can see wonderous things. Of course, there are plenty of places to buy gelato, too! You can visit churches and see all sorts of performances, too. Honestly, Rome is so big and has so many touristy things that I don't even know where to begin. I think I'll let you discover it by yourself!

Fontana dei Quattro Fiumi on Piazza Navona

CONCLUSION

Uh-oh, I can hear Elena and Aurora calling my name. I hope they don't want to play hairdressers again. Family! Well, it's true what they say: you can choose your friends but you can't choose your family. They might annoy me, but I still love them. Famiglia is very important to Italians. We live together and eat together, we're always together through thick and thin. I think about family a lot since Papà died. It doesn't matter whether your family is big or small, whether you have one parent or two, or whether you live with grandparents, cousins, or whoever. Family is important.

I know that one of the most stressful times for families is when they go on vacation! You often see tourists who look tired and are getting stressed with each other. If you're on holiday with your family, please be patient and remember you love them. Don't get stressed in the heat; it's easily done in the summer months. Try to adopt the Italian way of putting family first. Whether you're visiting museums, beaches, restaurants, country parks, or zoos, if you're doing it with family, it can turn into a wonderful adventure. Ah, there's my name again so I guess I'd better go and join my sisters. They drive me crazy, but we'll always be famiglia.

Which parts of Italy did you like the most and why?	What activities did you enjoy most and why?

Now, to our pop quiz! Good luck!

What is the population of Martina Franca?
(a)   50,000
(b)   65,000
(c)   95,000

(answer (a) — 50,000 people)

In July, how many hours of sunshine do they have every day in the town of Alghero, on the southern island of Sardinia?
(a)   7
(b)   9
(c)   11

(answer (c) — 11 hours of sunshine a day)

Which Roman God was supposedly the father of Romulus and Remus?
(a)   Neptune
(b)   Jupiter
(c)   Mars

(answer (c) — Mars)

How many UNESCO World Heritage Sites does Italy have?
(a)   38
(b)   46
(c)   54

(answer (c) — 54)

What is the name of the shop where you can buy an ice-cream in Italy?
(a)   Gelateria
(b)   Gelato Store
(c)   Ice-Cream Parlour

(answer (a) — Gelateria)

When was the last time that somebody was killed by an eruption at Mount Etna?
(a)   1943
(b)   1987
(c)   1992

(answer (b) — 1987. Two tourists were killed by a sudden explosion near the summit.)

How many recorded bird species are there in Italy?
(a)   Fewer than 200
(b)   About 300
(c)   More than 500

(answer (c) — More than 500)

Laurus nobilis is a type of evergreen tree that grows in Italy. What is its name in English?
(a)   Pine tree
(b)   Bay Laurel
(c)   Palm tree

(answer (b) — Bay Laurel)

Which of these cultural attractions in Italy entices the most visitors?
(a)   Colosseum, Palatino, and Roman Forum
(b)   Pompeii
(c)   Boboli Garden

(answer (a) — Colosseum, Palatino, and Roman Forum)

As a Catholic country, the Saints are important in Italy, but when is All Saints' Day?
(a)   January 1st
(b)   July 1st
(c)   November 1st

(answer (c) — November 1st)

I have thoroughly enjoyed this journey through France with you.
Feel free to visit us at www.dinobibi.com and check out our other titles!

Dinobibi Travel for Kids

Dinobibi History for Kids

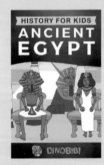
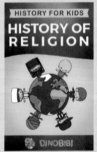

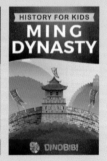

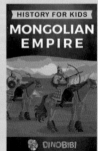